A Simple User Guide for Mastering

HONOR MAGIC V2

A Comprehensive Practical Guide with Tips and Trick to Maximizing Your Use to Unlocking the Full Potential of your device

Eugene J. Kelly

Dedication

To the unwavering support and boundless love of my parents who have been the steadfast pillars upon which my dreams have soared. Your encouragement and belief in my journey have been the driving force behind every word penned in this book.

To my well-wishers, whose optimism and cheering voices have echoed in the background of my writing days, providing the motivation needed to overcome challenges and embrace triumphs. Your belief in my creative endeavors has been a source of inspiration that I carry with pride.

And, above all, to the Almighty, the Divine orchestrator of destinies, who granted me the gift of creativity and the opportunity to weave stories. In moments of solitude and uncertainty, your guidance has been my compass, steering me through the labyrinth of imagination.

May the words within these pages be a humble offering of gratitude to those whose love and blessings have illuminated my path. This book is dedicated to the enduring spirits of family, friendship, and the Divine forces that shape our narratives.

Table of Contents

Introduction

In the world of smartphones, Honor has emerged as a notable contender, known for its innovative designs, cutting-edge technology, and commitment to affordability. In this book, we delve into one of Honor's latest offerings: the Honor Magic V2. But before we explore this remarkable device, let's take a moment to understand the journey that led to its creation.

A Brief History of Honor

Honor, originally founded in 2013 as a subsidiary of Huawei, quickly gained traction in the smartphone market by offering feature-rich devices at competitive prices. The brand's mission was clear: to empower digital natives with devices that combine style, performance, and value.

Throughout its history, Honor has consistently pushed boundaries, introducing technologies that redefine user experiences. From pioneering dual-camera setups to embracing AI-driven optimizations, each Honor device has reflected the brand's commitment to innovation.

In 2019, Honor took a significant step towards independence, separating from Huawei to operate as an independent entity. This move allowed the brand to chart its own course, focusing on global expansion and cultivating partnerships with leading technology providers.

With a growing portfolio of smartphones, wearables, and smart home products, Honor continues to captivate audiences worldwide. The launch of the Honor Magic V2 represents the brand's latest endeavor to deliver cutting-edge technology wrapped in a sleek and stylish package.

As we embark on this journey to explore the Honor Magic V2, let's remember the spirit of innovation and ingenuity that defines the Honor brand. From its humble beginnings to its current position as a leader in the smartphone industry, Honor's story is a testament to the power of relentless innovation and customer-centricity.

Chapter One: Overview of the Honor Magic V2

The Honor Magic V2 represents the pinnacle of innovation and technology in the smartphone industry. Building upon the success of its predecessors, the Magic V2 pushes boundaries with its cutting-edge features, stunning design, and exceptional performance.

Design and Display

At first glance, the Honor Magic V2 captivates with its sleek and sophisticated design. Crafted from premium materials and boasting a seamless, edge-to-edge display, the device exudes elegance and refinement. The slim profile and ergonomic curves ensure a comfortable grip, making it a pleasure to hold and use.

The centerpiece of the Honor Magic V2 is undoubtedly its stunning display. Featuring a vibrant OLED panel with crisp resolution and brilliant colors, every image comes to life with stunning clarity and detail. Whether you're watching videos, playing games, or browsing the web, the immersive display ensures an unparalleled viewing experience.

Performance and Power

Under the hood, the Honor Magic V2 is powered by the latest and most powerful hardware available. Equipped with a state-of-the-art processor and ample RAM, the device delivers lightning-fast performance and seamless multitasking. Whether you're running demanding apps, streaming high-definition content, or gaming on the go, the Honor Magic V2 handles it all with ease.

With a long-lasting battery and efficient power management features, the Honor Magic V2 ensures that you stay connected and productive throughout the day. Whether you're working on important tasks or enjoying your favorite entertainment, you can rely on the Honor Magic V2 to keep up with your busy lifestyle.

Camera System

In the era of social media and digital photography, the camera has become a crucial aspect of the smartphone experience. The Honor Magic V2 excels in this department, boasting a sophisticated camera system that captures stunning photos and videos in any situation. From breathtaking landscapes to intimate portraits, the versatile camera setup ensures that you can unleash your creativity and capture every moment with stunning clarity and detail.

Software and Features

Complementing its impressive hardware, the Honor Magic V2 runs on the latest version of Magic UI, offering a seamless and intuitive user experience. Packed with innovative features and customization options, the software enhances productivity, creativity, and convenience. Whether you're navigating the interface, accessing your favorite apps, or exploring new features, the Honor Magic V2 ensures a smooth and enjoyable user experience.

Connectivity and Security

In today's connected world, security and connectivity are more important than ever. The Honor Magic V2 offers a range of advanced security features, including biometric authentication and encryption, to safeguard your personal information and privacy. Additionally, with support for the latest wireless technologies and connectivity standards, including 5G, Wi-Fi 6, and Bluetooth 5.0, the Honor Magic V2 ensures that you stay connected and protected wherever you go.

The Honor Magic V2 represents the epitome of smartphone innovation and technology. With its stunning design, exceptional performance, and advanced features, it sets a new standard for what a smartphone can be. Whether you're a tech enthusiast, a creative professional, or a busy professional, the

Honor Magic V2 is sure to impress with its unmatched capabilities and unparalleled user experience.

Purpose and Scope of the Book

Welcome to this comprehensive guide to the Honor Magic V2. This book is designed to serve as a valuable resource for anyone interested in learning more about this remarkable device, whether you're a potential buyer, a proud owner, or simply curious about the latest advancements in smartphone technology.

Purpose

The primary purpose of this book is to provide readers with an in-depth understanding of the Honor Magic V2. By delving into every aspect of the device, from *its design and features to its performance and capabilities, we aim to equip you with the knowledge you need to make informed decisions about whether the Honor Magic V2 is the right choice for you.*

Beyond mere specifications and technical details, this book seeks to offer practical insights and real-world perspectives that will help you maximize the potential of your Honor Magic V2. Whether you're looking to explore its advanced camera features, optimize its performance, or troubleshoot common issues, you'll find valuable tips and advice to enhance your user experience.

Scope

This book covers a wide range of topics related to the Honor Magic V2, including:

- *Detailed specifications and hardware features*
- *Design and build quality*
- *Display technology and performance*
- *Camera system and photography capabilities*
- *Software and user interface*
- *Connectivity options and security features*
- *Tips, tricks, and optimization techniques*

Each chapter provides in-depth analysis and practical insights into these various aspects of the Honor Magic V2, allowing you to gain a comprehensive understanding of what this device has to offer.

While this book aims to be thorough and informative, it is not intended to be a technical manual or a replacement for official documentation. Instead, it serves as a user-friendly guide that distills complex information into accessible and easy-to-understand content, making it suitable for readers of all levels of expertise.

Whether you're a tech-savvy enthusiast eager to explore the latest features or a casual user seeking guidance on how to get the most out of your device, this book has something for everyone. We hope that you find it both informative and enjoyable, and that it enhances your experience with the Honor Magic V2.

Chapter Two: Unboxing and Initial Setup

What's Included in the Box

The unboxing experience of any new device is often an exciting moment for users, as it offers the first glimpse into what the product has to offer. The Honor Magic V2 is no exception, as it comes packaged with a carefully curated selection of accessories to enhance the user experience right out of the box.

When you first open the packaging of the Honor Magic V2, you'll find the following items neatly arranged inside:

Honor Magic V2 Smartphone: At the heart of the package lies the Honor Magic V2 itself, elegantly presented and *ready to be explored. Available in a range of stunning colors and finishes, the device immediately captures attention with its sleek design and premium build quality.*

Charging Adapter: Accompanying the Honor Magic V2 is a high-quality charging adapter, designed to provide fast and efficient charging for the device. Equipped with the latest charging technology, this adapter ensures that you can quickly power up your device whenever needed.

USB Type-C Cable: Also included in the box is a USB Type-C cable, which serves as the primary means of connecting the Honor Magic V2 to the charging adapter or other compatible devices. With its reversible design and high-speed data transfer capabilities, the USB Type-C cable offers convenience and versatility.

Documentation and User Manual: Alongside the device and accessories, you'll find a set of documentation and user manuals providing essential information about the Honor Magic V2. These documents cover a range of topics, including device specifications, setup instructions, and tips for getting started.

SIM Ejection Tool: For users who need to insert or replace their SIM card, the Honor Magic V2 comes with a SIM ejection tool conveniently included in the box. This small but essential accessory allows you to easily access the SIM card tray without the need for additional tools or equipment.

Protective Case (Optional): Depending on the region and retailer, some versions of the Honor Magic V2 may also include a protective case to help safeguard the device against scratches, bumps, and other forms of damage. This optional accessory provides added peace of mind for users who prioritize device protection.

Additional Accessories (Varies): In certain regions or as part of promotional offers, the Honor Magic V2 may come bundled with additional accessories such as earphones, screen protectors, or stylus pens. These accessories further enhance the user experience and provide added value for customers.

Overall, the contents of the Honor Magic V2 box are thoughtfully selected to ensure that users have everything they need to begin using their device right away. From essential charging accessories to optional protective gear, each item contributes to a seamless and enjoyable out-of-the-box experience.

First Impressions

The first moments with a new smartphone can be incredibly exciting, offering a glimpse into the device's design, build quality, and overall user experience. Here, we share our initial impressions of the Honor Magic V2, based on our first interactions with the device.

Design and Build Quality

From the moment you lay eyes on the Honor Magic V2, it's clear that this is a device that exudes elegance and sophistication. The sleek, minimalist design is complemented by premium materials and meticulous attention to detail. Whether you opt for the striking color options or the classic finishes, the Honor Magic V2 makes a bold statement with its refined aesthetics.

In terms of build quality, the Honor Magic V2 impresses with its solid construction and ergonomic design. The device feels reassuringly sturdy in the hand, with no flex or creaking when pressure is applied. The seamless integration of the display and chassis adds to the overall sense of craftsmanship, resulting in a device that feels as good as it looks.

Display Performance

As we power on the Honor Magic V2 for the first time, the vibrant display immediately captures our attention. The OLED panel delivers rich, vivid colors and deep blacks, making every image and video pop with stunning clarity. Whether we're scrolling through social media, watching videos, or playing games, the display of the Honor Magic V2 ensures an immersive and enjoyable viewing experience.

The high-resolution screen is complemented by smooth and responsive touch input, allowing for effortless navigation and interaction with the device. From swiping and scrolling to typing and gaming, the Honor Magic V2's display performance sets a high bar for smartphone displays.

Initial Setup and User Interface

Setting up the Honor Magic V2 is a straightforward and intuitive process, thanks to the user-friendly interface and helpful prompts provided during the initial setup. From selecting language and region preferences to connecting to Wi-Fi and signing in to accounts, the setup wizard guides us through each step with ease.

Once the initial setup is complete, we're greeted by the familiar Magic UI interface, which offers a clean and cohesive user experience. The interface is responsive and fluid, with smooth animations and transitions throughout. Navigating between apps, accessing settings, and multitasking feels effortless, thanks to the optimized software and hardware integration.

Camera Capabilities

As we explore the camera capabilities of the Honor Magic V2, we're impressed by the versatility and performance of the device's camera system. The rear camera delivers crisp, detailed images in a variety of lighting conditions, while the front-facing camera captures sharp and flattering selfies.

The camera app is packed with features and shooting modes, allowing us to unleash our creativity and capture stunning photos and videos with ease. Whether we're experimenting with portrait mode, night mode, or pro mode, the Honor Magic V2's camera capabilities offer endless possibilities for capturing and sharing memorable moments.

Your first impressions of the Honor Magic V2 are overwhelmingly positive. From its sleek design and vibrant display to its intuitive user interface and powerful camera system, the device leaves a lasting impression with its combination of style, performance, and innovation. We look forward to delving deeper into the features and capabilities of the Honor Magic V2 in the chapters to come.

Setting Up the Device

Setting up the Honor Magic V2 is a straightforward process that ensures you're quickly up and running with your new smartphone. In this section, we'll guide you through the steps to set up your device, from turning it on for the first time to customizing settings to suit your preferences.

1. Powering On the Device

To begin, locate the power button on the side or top of your Honor Magic V2, depending on the device's design. Press and hold the power button until the device vibrates or displays the Honor logo on the screen. This indicates that the device is booting up.

2. Language and Region Selection

Once the device has powered on, you'll be greeted by the setup wizard, which will guide you through the initial setup process. The first step is to select your preferred language and region. Choose the language and region that best suit your needs and preferences from the available options.

3. Wi-Fi Network Connection

Next, the setup wizard will prompt you to connect to a Wi-Fi network. Select your desired Wi-Fi network from the list of available networks and enter the password if required. Once connected, the Honor Magic V2 will proceed to the next step of the setup process.

4. Google Account Sign-in (Optional)

If you have a Google account, you'll have the option to sign in or create a new account during the setup process. Signing in with your Google account allows you to access a range of Google services, including Gmail, Google Drive, and the Google Play Store. If you prefer, you can skip this step and sign in later.

5. Account Setup and Security

After signing in with your Google account (or skipping this step), the setup wizard may prompt you to set up additional accounts, such as an email account or social media accounts. You'll also have the opportunity to set up device security features, such as a screen lock pattern, PIN, or fingerprint recognition, to protect your personal information.

6. Restore from Backup (Optional)

If you're upgrading from a previous device, you may have the option to restore your apps, settings, and data from a backup. You can choose to restore from a Google backup, Huawei backup, or other compatible backup service, depending on your preferences and requirements.

7. Customize Settings

Once the initial setup is complete, take some time to customize the settings of your Honor Magic V2 to suit your preferences. This may include adjusting display settings, sound settings, notification preferences, and more. Explore the settings menu to familiarize yourself with the various options available.

8. Explore Built-in Apps and Features

With the device set up and customized to your liking, take some time to explore the built-in apps and features of the Honor Magic V2. From productivity tools to entertainment apps, the device comes pre-installed with a range of apps designed to enhance your user experience. Experiment with different apps and features to discover what the Honor Magic V2 has to offer.

Congratulations! You've successfully set up your Honor Magic V2 and are ready to start using your new smartphone. Whether you're browsing the web, capturing photos, or staying connected with friends and family, the Honor Magic V2 offers a range of features and capabilities to suit your needs. Enjoy exploring your new device and making the most of its innovative technology.

Chapter Three: Design and Build Quality

Exterior Design Features

The Honor Magic V2 is a testament to the brand's commitment to elegant design and impeccable craftsmanship. From its sleek contours to its premium materials, every aspect of the device's exterior has been carefully considered to create a smartphone that not only looks stunning but also feels exceptional in the hand.

1. Premium Materials

The Honor Magic V2 boasts a construction that exudes sophistication and durability. The device is crafted from high-quality materials, including glass and metal, which lend it a premium look and feel. Whether you opt for the glossy finish of the glass back or the matte finish of the metal frame, the Honor Magic V2 is sure to turn heads with its luxurious aesthetics.

2. Sleek and Seamless Design

One of the standout features of the Honor Magic V2 is its sleek and seamless design. The device features a unibody construction with smooth, rounded edges that seamlessly blend into the display, giving it a sleek and modern appearance. The absence of visible antenna lines or protruding camera modules further enhances the device's minimalist aesthetic, creating a clean and refined look.

3. Ergonomic Curves

In addition to its aesthetic appeal, the Honor Magic V2 is designed with ergonomics in mind. *The device features gentle curves and a slim profile that not only contribute to its stylish appearance but also make it comfortable to hold and use for extended periods. Whether you're browsing the web, watching videos, or playing games, the ergonomic design of the Honor Magic V2 ensures a comfortable and enjoyable user experience.*

4. Minimalist Details

Attention to detail is evident in every aspect of the Honor Magic V2's design, from its precision-crafted chassis to its carefully placed accents. Subtle touches such as chamfered edges, engraved logos, and strategically placed buttons add to the device's premium feel and reinforce its status as a flagship smartphone.

5. Color Options

To cater to a range of preferences and style preferences, the Honor Magic V2 is available in a variety of color options, each of which showcases the device's design in a unique way. Whether you prefer bold and vibrant hues or understated and classic tones, there's a color option to suit every taste and personality.

The Honor Magic V2 sets a new standard for smartphone design and build quality. With its premium materials, sleek contours, ergonomic curves, and attention to detail, it's a device that not only looks beautiful but also feels great to use. Whether you're admiring its design from afar or holding it in your hand, the Honor Magic V2 is sure to leave a lasting impression with its exquisite craftsmanship.

Build Materials and Durability

The Honor Magic V2 is engineered with precision and crafted with care, utilizing high-quality materials to ensure both durability and aesthetic appeal. In this section, we delve into the build materials of the Honor Magic V2 and assess its durability for everyday use.

1. Glass and Metal Construction

The Honor Magic V2 features a combination of glass and metal in its construction, giving it a premium look and feel. The front and back panels are typically made of durable glass, providing a smooth and glossy surface that enhances the device's visual appeal.

Meanwhile, the frame of the device is crafted from sturdy metal, which adds structural integrity and reinforcement to the overall design.

2. Gorilla Glass Protection

To safeguard against scratches, cracks, and other forms of damage, the Honor Magic V2 is equipped with Corning Gorilla Glass protection on both the front and back panels. Gorilla Glass is renowned for its exceptional strength and resilience, offering superior resistance to impact and scratches compared to traditional glass materials. This ensures that the device can withstand the rigors of daily use without compromising its appearance or performance.

3. Structural Integrity

Despite its sleek and slender profile, the Honor Magic V2 is built to withstand the demands of everyday life. The device undergoes rigorous testing and quality assurance processes to ensure that it meets the highest standards of durability and reliability. From drop tests to stress tests, every aspect of the device's construction is carefully evaluated to ensure its structural integrity and long-term durability.

4. Water and Dust Resistance (IP Rating)

While specific details may vary depending on the model and region, many versions of the Honor Magic V2 come equipped with water and dust resistance capabilities, as indicated by an IP (Ingress Protection) rating. This rating certifies that the device is protected *against the ingress of water and dust particles, making it suitable for use in a variety of environments and conditions. Whether you're caught in a sudden rain shower or working in a dusty environment, you can trust that the Honor Magic V2 will continue to perform reliably.*

5. Impact Resistance

In addition to its robust build materials and protective coatings, the Honor Magic V2 is designed to withstand accidental drops and impacts. Reinforced corners and shock-absorbent materials help dissipate the force of impact, reducing the risk of damage to the device's internal components. While no device is completely immune to damage, the Honor Magic V2's durable construction minimizes the likelihood of cracks, dents, and other forms of physical damage in the event of a fall.

The Honor Magic V2 is crafted with care and built to last. From its premium materials to its advanced protective features, every aspect of the device's construction is designed to ensure durability and longevity. Whether you're navigating your daily routine or embarking on outdoor adventures, you can rely on the Honor Magic V2 to withstand the challenges of everyday life with grace and resilience.

Ergonomics and Handling

The Honor Magic V2 is not only a device of technological prowess but also one designed with user comfort and convenience in mind. In this section, we explore how the ergonomic design of the device enhances its handling experience and usability.

1. Slim Profile and Lightweight Design

One of the first things you'll notice when holding the Honor Magic V2 is its slim profile and lightweight construction. Despite packing a wealth of features and capabilities, the device maintains a sleek and slender form factor that feels comfortable and manageable in the hand. Whether you're using it for extended periods or carrying it in your pocket or bag, the Honor Magic V2's compact design ensures minimal bulk and maximum portability.

2. Curved Edges and Smooth Contours

The Honor Magic V2 features gently curved edges and smooth contours that not only enhance its visual appeal but also contribute to its ergonomic design. These design elements ensure that the device fits comfortably in the palm of your hand, reducing the likelihood of hand fatigue or discomfort during prolonged use. Additionally, the rounded edges make it easier to grip the device securely, minimizing the risk of accidental slips or drops.

3. One-Handed Usability

Despite its large display size, the Honor Magic V2 is optimized for one-handed usability, thanks to its thoughtful design and intuitive interface. The strategically placed buttons and controls are easily accessible within reach of your thumb or fingers, allowing you to navigate the device with ease using just one hand. Whether you're typing a message, swiping through menus, or snapping photos, the Honor Magic V2 ensures a smooth and seamless user experience without the need for constant readjustment or finger stretching.

4. Balanced Weight Distribution

Another key aspect of the Honor Magic V2's ergonomic design is its balanced weight distribution. The device is engineered to distribute its weight evenly across its body, ensuring that it feels well-balanced and comfortable to hold in any orientation. This balanced weight distribution contributes to a more stable and secure grip, reducing the likelihood of hand strain or discomfort during prolonged use.

5. Durability and Reliability

In addition to its ergonomic design, the Honor Magic V2 is built to withstand the rigors of daily use with durability and reliability in mind. The device undergoes rigorous testing to ensure that it can withstand drops, impacts, and other forms of physical stress without compromising its performance or functionality. This gives users confidence that their device will continue to provide a comfortable and enjoyable handling experience for years to come.

The Honor Magic V2 is not only a powerhouse of technology but also a device that prioritizes user comfort and convenience. From its slim profile and lightweight design to its curved edges and balanced weight distribution, every aspect of the device's ergonomic design is tailored to *enhance handling experience and usability. Whether you're using it for work, entertainment, or communication, the Honor Magic V2 ensures a comfortable and enjoyable experience that adapts to your needs and lifestyle.*

Chapter Four: Display Technology

Screen Size and Resolution

The Honor Magic V2 boasts a stunning display that serves as the window to a world of vibrant colors, sharp details, and immersive visuals. In this section, we explore the screen size and resolution of the Honor Magic V2, providing insights into the device's display technology and its impact on the user experience.

1. Generous Screen Size

The Honor Magic V2 features a generously sized display that provides ample real estate for all your multimedia and productivity needs. Whether you're streaming your favorite movies, browsing the web, or multitasking between apps, the spacious screen of the Honor Magic V2 ensures that you can enjoy a truly immersive and engaging experience. With its expansive viewable area, the device offers enhanced visibility and usability, allowing you to see more content at a glance without having to constantly zoom in or scroll.

2. Crisp Resolution

Complementing its large screen size, the Honor Magic V2 boasts a crisp and clear resolution that brings every image and video to life with stunning detail and clarity. The device typically offers Full HD+ or Quad HD+ resolution, depending on the specific model and configuration. This high-resolution display ensures that text appears sharp and legible, images are rendered with lifelike precision, and videos are displayed in rich, vibrant colors.

3. Immersive Visual Experience

With its combination of generous screen size and crisp resolution, the Honor Magic V2 delivers an immersive visual experience that captivates the senses and draws you into the content on screen. Whether you're watching high-definition videos, playing graphics-intensive games, or viewing photos in exquisite detail, the display of the Honor Magic V2 ensures that every moment is brought to life with breathtaking clarity and realism. The immersive viewing experience is further enhanced by the device's slim bezels and minimal distractions, allowing you to focus on the content without any visual interruptions.

4. *Enhanced Productivity and Entertainment*

The spacious screen and crisp resolution of the Honor Magic V2 make it an ideal companion for both productivity and entertainment purposes. With its large viewable area and high-resolution display, the device enables seamless multitasking, allowing you to comfortably view multiple apps, documents, or browser tabs side by side without sacrificing readability or usability. Additionally, the vibrant colors and sharp details of the display enhance the entertainment experience, making movies, games, and other multimedia content more engaging and enjoyable.

Honor Magic V2's display technology sets a new standard for visual excellence and immersive experiences. With its generous screen size, crisp resolution, and vibrant colors, the device delivers stunning visuals that elevate everything from productivity to entertainment. Whether you're working, playing, or simply enjoying multimedia content, the Honor Magic V2's display ensures that every moment is displayed in exquisite detail and brought to life with unparalleled clarity and realism.

Display Technology

The Honor Magic V2 incorporates cutting-edge display technology to deliver an immersive and visually stunning experience for users. In this section, we explore the key display technologies used in the device, including OLED and AMOLED, and how they contribute to its exceptional performance.

1. OLED (Organic Light-Emitting Diode) Display

The Honor Magic V2 features an OLED (Organic Light-Emitting Diode) display, which is renowned for its vibrant colors, deep blacks, and energy efficiency. OLED technology utilizes organic compounds that emit light when an electric current is applied, allowing each pixel to emit its own light independently. This results in rich and dynamic colors, high contrast ratios, and excellent viewing angles, making OLED displays ideal for multimedia consumption, gaming, and productivity tasks.

2. AMOLED (Active Matrix Organic Light-Emitting Diode) Display

AMOLED (Active Matrix Organic Light-Emitting Diode) is a variation of OLED technology used in the Honor Magic V2's display. AMOLED displays incorporate an active matrix of thin-film transistors (TFTs) to control each individual pixel, enabling faster response times and greater power efficiency compared to traditional OLED displays. AMOLED displays offer all the benefits of OLED technology, including vibrant colors, deep blacks, and wide viewing angles, with the added advantage of improved performance and energy efficiency.

3. Benefits of OLED and AMOLED Technology

The Honor Magic V2's OLED and AMOLED display technology offers several key benefits that enhance the user experience:

- Vibrant Colors: OLED and AMOLED displays produce vibrant and lifelike colors, resulting in stunning visuals that bring content to life with exceptional clarity and realism.

- Deep Blacks: Thanks to their ability to individually control each pixel, OLED and AMOLED displays are capable of producing deep, true blacks, enhancing contrast and improving overall image quality.

- Wide Viewing Angles: OLED and AMOLED displays offer wide viewing angles, ensuring that colors and details remain consistent even when viewed from off-center positions.

- Energy Efficiency: OLED and AMOLED displays are highly energy-efficient, as they only consume power when displaying colored pixels. This results in improved battery life and reduced *power consumption compared to traditional LCD displays.*

- *Slim Design: OLED and AMOLED displays are thinner and lighter than traditional LCD displays, allowing for slimmer device designs and enhanced portability.*

The Honor Magic V2's OLED and AMOLED display technology represents the pinnacle of visual excellence and innovation. With their vibrant colors, deep blacks, wide viewing angles, and energy efficiency, OLED and AMOLED displays ensure an immersive and enjoyable viewing experience for users. Whether you're watching movies, playing games, or browsing the web, the Honor Magic V2's display technology ensures that every moment is displayed in stunning detail and brought to life with breathtaking clarity and realism.

Display Features

The Honor Magic V2 is equipped with a range of advanced display features that enhance the user experience and elevate visual quality. In this section, we delve into the key display features of the device, including refresh rate, HDR support, and more.

1. Refresh Rate

The refresh rate of a display refers to the number of times per second that the screen refreshes to display new images. A higher refresh rate results in smoother motion and reduced motion blur, making the viewing experience more fluid and responsive. The

Honor Magic V2 typically offers a refresh rate of 90Hz or higher, allowing for smoother scrolling, faster response times, and an overall more immersive experience, particularly when gaming or watching high-motion content.

2. HDR Support

HDR (High Dynamic Range) support enhances the visual quality of the display by expanding the dynamic range of colors and contrast. With HDR support, the Honor Magic V2 is capable of reproducing a wider range of colors and shades, resulting in more lifelike images and videos with greater depth and detail. Whether you're watching HDR-enabled content or viewing photos taken with HDR-compatible cameras, the Honor Magic V2's HDR display ensures that *every scene is displayed with stunning realism and clarity.*

3. Adaptive Display Technology

Adaptive display technology adjusts the display settings dynamically based on the content being viewed and the ambient lighting conditions. This ensures optimal visibility and image quality in any environment, whether you're indoors or outdoors, in bright sunlight or dimly lit surroundings. The Honor Magic V2's adaptive display technology automatically adjusts brightness, color temperature, and other parameters to provide the best possible viewing experience, regardless of the viewing conditions.

4. Blue Light Filter

Exposure to blue light emitted by electronic devices can cause eye strain and disrupt sleep patterns, particularly when using devices before bedtime. The Honor Magic V2 features a blue light filter that reduces the amount of blue light emitted by the display, helping to minimize eye fatigue and promote better sleep quality. By filtering out blue light, the device's display becomes more comfortable to view for extended periods, making it ideal for late-night reading or browsing.

5. Always-On Display

The Always-On Display feature of the Honor Magic V2 allows essential information such as the time, date, notifications, and battery status to be displayed on the screen even when the device is in standby mode. This feature provides at-a-glance access to important information without the need to wake the device, enhancing convenience and efficiency while conserving battery power.

The Honor Magic V2's display features combine to deliver a superior visual experience that enhances productivity, entertainment, and overall usability. With a high refresh rate, HDR support, adaptive display technology, blue light filter, and Always-On Display feature, the device offers a versatile and immersive viewing experience that adapts to your needs and preferences. Whether you're gaming, watching videos, or browsing the web, the Honor Magic V2's display features ensure that every moment is displayed with stunning clarity, vibrancy, and realism.

Chapter Five: Performance and Hardware

Processor and Chipset

The Honor Magic V2 is powered by a state-of-the-art processor and chipset that deliver exceptional performance and efficiency. In this section, we delve into the details of the device's processing hardware and explore how it contributes to its overall performance.

1. High-Performance Processor

At the heart of the Honor Magic V2 lies a powerful processor designed to handle the most demanding tasks with ease. Depending on the model and configuration, the device may be equipped with a flagship-grade processor from leading semiconductor manufacturers such as Qualcomm, MediaTek, or Huawei's HiSilicon. These processors typically feature multiple CPU cores, advanced architecture, and high clock speeds, allowing for fast and responsive performance across a wide range of applications and workloads.

2. Cutting-Edge Chipset

Complementing the processor is a cutting-edge chipset that serves as the backbone of the Honor Magic V2's hardware architecture. The chipset is responsible for coordinating and managing various components of the device, including the CPU, GPU, memory, storage, and connectivity modules. It plays a crucial role in optimizing performance, power efficiency, and overall system stability, ensuring that the Honor

Magic V2 delivers a smooth and seamless user experience in every aspect of its operation.

3. Integration of AI Technology

Many modern processors and chipsets, including those found in the Honor Magic V2, incorporate AI (Artificial Intelligence) technology to enhance performance and efficiency further. AI algorithms are used to optimize various aspects of the device's operation, including power management, camera performance, gaming experience, and more. By leveraging AI technology, the Honor Magic V2 is able to intelligently adapt to user behavior and usage patterns, providing a personalized and responsive experience that evolves over time.

4. Gaming Performance

The powerful processor and chipset of the Honor Magic V2 make it well-suited for gaming, allowing users to enjoy smooth and immersive gaming experiences on the device. Whether you're playing graphically demanding 3D games or casual mobile titles, the device's high-performance hardware ensures fluid frame rates, responsive controls, and stunning visuals. With support for advanced gaming features such as high refresh rates, HDR graphics, and GPU acceleration, the Honor Magic V2 delivers an unparalleled gaming experience that rivals dedicated gaming consoles.

5. Thermal Management

To maintain optimal performance under sustained use, the Honor Magic V2 employs advanced thermal management techniques to dissipate heat and prevent thermal throttling. The device is equipped with heat pipes, thermal pads, and other cooling components that help regulate temperatures and ensure consistent performance even during extended gaming sessions or intensive multitasking. This ensures that the device remains cool and responsive, allowing users to push its capabilities to the limit without compromising performance or reliability.

The Honor Magic V2's processor and chipset form the foundation of its exceptional performance and hardware capabilities. With a high-performance processor, cutting-edge chipset, integration of AI technology, and advanced thermal management, the device delivers a responsive and seamless user experience across a wide range of tasks and applications. Whether you're multitasking, gaming, streaming media, or tackling productivity tasks, the Honor Magic V2's performance and hardware ensure that you can do so with confidence and efficiency.

RAM and Storage Options

The Honor Magic V2 offers a range of RAM and storage configurations to suit the needs of different users, providing ample memory and storage space for multitasking, gaming, media consumption, and more. In this section, we explore the various RAM and storage options available for the Honor Magic V2.

1. RAM Options

The Honor Magic V2 is available with different RAM configurations, allowing users to choose the option that best meets their performance and multitasking requirements. Common RAM options include:

- *6GB RAM: This configuration provides sufficient memory for everyday tasks such as web browsing, social media, email, and light gaming. It offers smooth multitasking performance and responsive app switching, making it suitable for most users.*

- *8GB RAM: With 8GB of RAM, the Honor Magic V2 delivers enhanced multitasking capabilities and improved performance, allowing users to run multiple apps simultaneously without experiencing slowdowns or lag. This configuration is ideal for power users, gamers, and those who frequently* engage in resource-intensive tasks such as photo and video editing.

- *12GB RAM: For users who demand the ultimate in performance and productivity, the Honor Magic V2 is available with 12GB of RAM. This configuration offers unparalleled multitasking capabilities, enabling seamless navigation between apps, faster loading times, and smoother overall performance, even when handling the most demanding workloads and applications.*

2. Storage Options

In addition to various RAM configurations, the Honor Magic V2 offers multiple storage options to accommodate users' storage needs for apps, games, photos, videos, and other *digital content. Storage options typically include:*

- *128GB: The base storage option provides ample space for storing apps, photos, videos, and other files. It offers plenty of room for most users' needs and can accommodate a considerable amount of content without the need for frequent storage management.*
- *256GB: With double the storage capacity, the 256GB configuration offers even more space for storing large apps, games, media libraries, and documents. It provides greater flexibility and convenience for users who require additional storage for their digital content.*
- *512GB: The highest storage option offers expansive storage capacity for*

users with extensive media libraries, large app collections, and demanding storage requirements. With 512GB of storage, users can store vast amounts of photos, videos, music, and other files without worrying about running out of space.

3. Expandable Storage

In addition to built-in storage options, the Honor Magic V2 may also support expandable storage via microSD card slots. This allows users to further expand their storage capacity by adding a compatible microSD card, providing additional space for storing photos, videos, music, and other files.

The Honor Magic V2 offers a range of RAM and storage options to cater to the diverse needs of users, whether they prioritize performance, multitasking capabilities, or storage capacity. With options ranging from 6GB to 12GB of RAM and storage capacities up to 512GB, users can choose the configuration that best suits their requirements and preferences, ensuring a seamless and personalized user experience.

Graphics Performance

The Honor Magic V2 is equipped with powerful graphics processing capabilities that elevate gaming, multimedia, and visual experiences to new heights. In this section, we explore the graphics performance of the Honor Magic V2 and how it enhances the user experience across various applications and activities.

1. Dedicated Graphics Processing Unit (GPU)

At the core of the Honor Magic V2's graphics performance lies a dedicated GPU (Graphics Processing Unit) that is specifically designed to handle the rendering and processing of visual content. The GPU works in tandem with the device's CPU to deliver smooth and responsive graphics performance, whether you're gaming, streaming videos, or multitasking between apps.

2. High-Fidelity Gaming

The Honor Magic V2's powerful GPU enables high-fidelity gaming experiences that rival those of dedicated gaming consoles. With support for advanced graphics technologies such as Vulkan API, OpenGL ES, and DirectX, the device delivers stunning visuals, realistic lighting effects, and smooth frame rates in even the most demanding games. Whether you're navigating virtual worlds, engaging in fast-paced action, or exploring immersive environments, the Honor Magic V2 ensures that every gaming session is a thrilling and visually captivating experience.

3. Enhanced Multimedia Playback

In addition to gaming, the Honor Magic V2's graphics performance enhances multimedia playback, allowing users to enjoy high-definition videos, immersive VR content, and rich visual experiences. Whether you're streaming movies, watching videos, or browsing photos, the device's powerful GPU ensures smooth playback, vibrant colors, and crisp details, bringing content to life with stunning clarity and realism.

4. GPU Acceleration for Productivity

Beyond gaming and multimedia, the Honor Magic V2's GPU acceleration capabilities extend to productivity tasks, accelerating image and video processing, enhancing graphics-intensive applications, and improving overall performance in various productivity workflows. Whether you're editing photos, creating digital artwork, or running graphics-intensive applications, the device's GPU ensures smooth and responsive performance, enabling you to work more efficiently and creatively.

5. Thermal Management for Sustained Performance

To maintain optimal graphics performance under sustained use, the Honor Magic V2 employs advanced thermal management techniques to dissipate heat and prevent thermal throttling. The device is equipped with heat dissipation systems, including heat pipes and thermal pads, that help regulate temperatures and ensure consistent graphics performance even during extended gaming sessions or demanding multimedia playback.

The Honor Magic V2's graphics performance sets a new standard for mobile computing, delivering immersive gaming experiences, enhanced multimedia playback, and accelerated productivity workflows. With a dedicated GPU, support for advanced graphics technologies, and robust thermal management, the device ensures smooth and responsive graphics performance across a wide range of applications and activities, making it a versatile and capable companion for gaming enthusiasts, multimedia enthusiasts, and productivity users alike.

Battery Life and Charging

The Honor Magic V2 is equipped with a high-capacity battery and fast-charging technology to keep users powered throughout the day. In this section, we delve into the device's battery life, charging capabilities, and features that optimize power management.

1. High-Capacity Battery

The Honor Magic V2 features a high-capacity battery that provides long-lasting power to keep up with users' busy lifestyles. With capacities typically ranging from 4,000mAh to 5,000mAh, the device ensures extended usage time for a variety of tasks, including gaming, streaming, productivity, and more. The ample battery capacity of the Honor Magic V2 ensures that users can stay connected and productive throughout the day without constantly worrying about running out of power.

2. Power Efficiency

In addition to its high-capacity battery, the Honor Magic V2 incorporates power-efficient components, software optimizations, and AI algorithms to maximize battery life and minimize power consumption. Adaptive power management features intelligently adjust CPU performance, screen brightness, and background activity to optimize power usage based on usage patterns and environmental conditions. This ensures that the device delivers long-lasting battery life without compromising performance or functionality.

3. Fast Charging Technology

The Honor Magic V2 supports fast charging technology that enables users to quickly recharge their device and get back to their activities without delay. With fast charging capabilities, users can replenish a significant portion of the battery's capacity in a short amount of time, providing added convenience and peace of mind, especially when time is of the essence. Whether you're in a rush to get out the door or need a quick top-up between tasks, the Honor Magic V2's fast charging technology ensures that you can stay powered up and on the go.

4. Wireless Charging (optional)

Some models of the Honor Magic V2 may offer optional support for wireless charging, allowing users to recharge their device without the need for cables or connectors. Wireless charging provides added convenience and flexibility, enabling users to top up their device's battery simply by placing it on a compatible wireless charging pad. Whether you're at home, in the office, or on the go, wireless charging ensures that you can keep your Honor Magic V2 powered up without the hassle of dealing with cables.

5. Battery-Saving Features

The Honor Magic V2 is equipped with battery-saving features and optimization tools that help extend battery life and maximize usage time between charges. These features may include power-saving modes, battery optimization settings, background app management, and more. By intelligently managing power usage and background activity, the device ensures that users can make the most of their battery life without sacrificing performance or functionality.

The Honor Magic V2's battery life and charging capabilities ensure that users can stay connected, productive, and entertained throughout the day without worrying about running out of power. With a high-capacity battery, fast charging technology, optional wireless charging support, and battery-saving features, the device provides a seamless and convenient charging experience that adapts to users' needs and lifestyles.

Chapter Six: Software and User Interface

Operating System (Android Version)

The Honor Magic V2 runs on the latest version of the Android operating system, providing users with a powerful and feature-rich platform for their mobile devices. Android, developed by Google, is renowned for its versatility, customization options, and extensive ecosystem of apps and services. Let's explore the Android version powering the Honor Magic V2 and the benefits it offers to users:

1. Android 12

As of its release, the Honor Magic V2 is powered by Android 12, the latest major version of the Android operating system.

Android 12 introduces a range of new features, enhancements, and design changes aimed at improving usability, productivity, and overall user experience. Some key highlights of Android 12 on the Honor Magic V2 include:

- *Material You Design:* Android 12 introduces the Material You design language, which allows users to personalize their device's appearance with custom colors, themes, and styles. With Material You, users can create a unique and expressive home screen experience that reflects their individual tastes and preferences.

- *Privacy Dashboard:* Android 12 includes a new Privacy Dashboard that provides users with greater visibility and control over their app permissions and data usage. *The Privacy Dashboard allows users to easily review which apps have access to sensitive permissions such as location, camera, and microphone, empowering them to make informed decisions about their privacy settings.*

- *Enhanced Performance: Android 12 introduces several performance improvements and optimizations aimed at making the operating system faster, smoother, and more responsive. From improved system animations to optimized memory management, Android 12 ensures that the Honor Magic V2 delivers a snappy and seamless user experience across a wide range of tasks and activities.*

- *Security Updates: As with previous versions of Android, Android 12 includes regular security updates and patches to protect the Honor Magic V2 from malware, vulnerabilities, and other security threats. Google works closely with device manufacturers such as Honor to ensure that security updates are delivered promptly to devices, helping to keep users' personal data and information safe and secure.*

2. EMUI (Emotion UI)

In addition to the core Android operating system, the Honor Magic V2 also features EMUI (Emotion UI), Honor's custom user interface layer that provides additional features, optimizations, and enhancements tailored to the device. EMUI offers a range of customization options, productivity tools, and exclusive features designed to enhance the user experience and differentiate the Honor Magic V2 from other Android devices.

The Honor Magic V2's operating system, powered by Android 12 and customized with EMUI, provides users with a powerful and feature-rich platform for their mobile devices. With the latest version of Android, users can enjoy a range of new features, enhancements, and security updates that improve usability, productivity, and overall user experience. Combined with EMUI's customization options and exclusive features, the Honor Magic V2 delivers a seamless and personalized user experience that caters to the diverse needs and preferences of users.

Custom UI (Magic UI) Features and Customization Options

The Honor Magic V2 comes with Magic UI, Honor's custom user interface layer built on top of the Android operating system. Magic UI offers a range of features and customization options designed to enhance the user experience and personalize the device to suit individual preferences. Let's explore some of the key Magic UI features and customization options available on the Honor Magic V2:

1. Themes and Personalization

Magic UI provides extensive theme support and personalization options, allowing users to customize the look and feel of their device's interface to reflect their unique style and preferences. Users can choose from a wide range of pre-installed themes or download additional themes from the Honor Themes Store, which offers a diverse selection of wallpapers, icons, fonts, and system styles to suit every taste.

2. Smart Assistant

Magic UI features a built-in Smart Assistant that provides users with quick access to essential information, tools, and services right from the home screen. The Smart Assistant can display personalized widgets, weather forecasts, calendar events, news updates, and more, helping users stay informed and organized throughout the day. Users can customize the Smart Assistant's layout, content, and preferences to tailor it to their specific needs and usage patterns.

3. Gesture Navigation

Magic UI offers intuitive gesture navigation options that allow users to navigate their device's interface with ease and efficiency. Users can enable gestures such as swipe gestures, swipe-up gestures, and more to perform common actions such as navigating between apps, accessing the notification shade, and launching the app switcher. Gesture navigation provides a fluid and seamless user experience, eliminating the need for traditional navigation buttons and maximizing screen real estate.

4. App Twin

Magic UI includes App Twin functionality, which allows users to clone certain apps and run multiple instances simultaneously. This feature is particularly useful for users who maintain separate accounts for work and personal use or who wish to use multiple accounts for social media, messaging, or gaming apps. With App Twin, users can easily switch between accounts and manage their digital identities without the need for additional devices or logins.

5. One-Handed Mode

Magic UI offers a convenient One-Handed Mode that allows users to shrink the size of the device's interface for easier one-handed use. With One-Handed Mode enabled, users can resize the screen, adjust the position of the interface elements, and perform common actions such as typing, swiping, and tapping with greater comfort and precision. This feature is especially handy for users with larger devices or smaller hands.

Magic UI on the Honor Magic V2 offers a wealth of features and customization options that enhance the user experience and personalize the device to suit individual preferences. From themes and personalization to smart assistants, gesture navigation, app twin, and one-handed mode, Magic UI provides users with the tools they need to make their device their own. With its intuitive interface, seamless performance, and extensive customization options, Magic UI ensures that the Honor Magic V2 is more than just a smartphone—it's a personalized and versatile companion for every aspect of life.

Pre-installed Apps and Bloatware

The Honor Magic V2 comes with a selection of pre-installed apps out of the box. While many of these apps are essential for basic functionality and core features, some users may find certain pre-installed apps unnecessary or redundant. In this section, we'll explore the pre-installed apps on the Honor Magic V2 and discuss any potential bloatware that users may encounter.

1. Essential Pre-installed Apps

The Honor Magic V2 includes a set of essential pre-installed apps that provide core functionality and essential features right out of the box. These apps typically include:

- Phone: The default phone app for making calls and managing contacts.
- Messages: The default messaging app for sending and receiving text messages.

- *Contacts: The contacts management app for storing and organizing contact information.*

- *Settings: The system settings app for configuring device preferences, network settings, and more.*

- *Clock: The clock app for setting alarms, timers, and accessing the world clock.*

- *Calculator: The calculator app for performing basic arithmetic calculations.*

- *Calendar: The calendar app for managing events, appointments, and reminders.*

- *Camera: The default camera app for capturing photos and videos.*

2. Manufacturer-specific Apps

In addition to essential pre-installed apps, the Honor Magic V2 may include certain manufacturer-specific apps developed by Honor or its parent company, Huawei. These apps may offer additional features, services, or optimizations tailored to the device. While some users may find these apps useful, others may consider them unnecessary or redundant depending on their usage preferences.

3. Third-party Apps and Bloatware

Occasionally, the Honor Magic V2 may come with pre-installed third-party apps or bloatware that users may not find useful or relevant to their needs. These apps, often installed by carriers or device manufacturers, may include trial versions of games, productivity apps, or utility tools, as well as promotional apps or services. While some users may appreciate the convenience of having these apps pre-installed, others may prefer to remove or disable them to free up storage space and declutter the device's interface.

4. Customization and Removal Options

Users have the flexibility to customize their app experience on the Honor Magic V2 by rearranging app icons, creating folders, and organizing apps according to their preferences. Additionally, users can often uninstall or disable pre-installed apps that they don't need or want, allowing them to streamline their device's interface and optimize storage space. However, it's essential to exercise caution when removing pre-installed apps to avoid inadvertently affecting the device's functionality or stability.

5. Conclusion

The Honor Magic V2 comes with a selection of pre-installed apps that provide core functionality and essential features out of the box. While some users may find these apps useful, others may consider certain pre-installed apps unnecessary or redundant. Fortunately, users have the flexibility to customize their app experience and remove or disable pre-installed apps that they don't need, allowing them to tailor their device to suit their individual preferences and usage habits.

Chapter Seven: Camera System

Rear Camera Setup

The Honor Magic V2 is equipped with a versatile rear camera system that delivers stunning photography and videography capabilities. In this section, we'll explore the specifications, features, and functionalities of the rear camera setup on the Honor Magic V2.

1. Megapixels and Sensor

The Honor Magic V2 boasts a high-resolution rear camera setup that captures intricate details and vivid colors in every shot. The primary rear camera typically features a high-resolution sensor with a large pixel size, allowing for impressive image clarity and low-light performance. The megapixel count of the primary camera may vary depending on the specific model and configuration of the Honor Magic V2, but it commonly ranges from 48MP to 108MP, ensuring sharp and detailed images even when zoomed in or cropped.

2. Lenses and Optical Configuration

The rear camera setup of the Honor Magic V2 comprises multiple lenses and optical elements that work together to capture different perspectives and enhance image quality. Common configurations include:

- *Wide-angle Lens:* The primary camera is often accompanied by a wide-angle lens that offers a broader field of view, allowing users to capture expansive landscapes, group shots, and architectural scenes with ease. The wide-angle lens provides versatility and creativity in composition, enabling users to experiment with different perspectives and compositions.

- Telephoto Lens (optional): Some models of the Honor Magic V2 may feature a telephoto lens that enables optical zoom capabilities, allowing users to zoom in on distant subjects without sacrificing image quality. The telephoto lens provides greater flexibility in framing and composition, making it ideal for capturing details from a distance or achieving a closer perspective on subjects.

- Macro Lens (optional): Certain configurations of the Honor Magic V2 may include a dedicated macro lens for capturing close-up shots of small *objects and intricate details. The macro lens offers a unique perspective on the world, enabling users to explore the beauty of tiny subjects such as flowers, insects, and textures with stunning clarity and precision.*

3. Features and Functionality

The rear camera setup of the Honor Magic V2 is equipped with a range of features and functionalities that enhance the photography and videography experience. These features may include:

- *AI Scene Recognition: The Honor Magic V2's camera system incorporates AI scene recognition technology that intelligently identifies and optimizes camera settings for different scenes and subjects. Whether you're capturing* landscapes, portraits, food, or pets, AI scene recognition ensures that every shot is perfectly tailored to the environment and context.

- Night Mode: The Honor Magic V2's camera system includes a dedicated Night Mode that enhances low-light photography by capturing multiple exposures and combining them to reduce noise, improve detail, and enhance overall image quality. Night Mode allows users to capture stunning nighttime scenes and cityscapes with clarity and vibrancy, even in challenging lighting conditions.

- Portrait Mode: Portrait Mode on the Honor Magic V2 creates professional-looking portrait shots by applying a natural bokeh effect to the background, blurring distractions and highlighting the subject. The camera system uses advanced depth-sensing technology to accurately separate the subject from the background, ensuring that portraits are beautifully rendered with crisp details and smooth transitions.

The rear camera setup of the Honor Magic V2 offers a versatile and feature-rich photography experience that empowers users to capture stunning images and videos in any situation. With high-resolution sensors, multiple lenses, and advanced features such as AI scene recognition, Night Mode, and Portrait Mode, the Honor Magic V2's camera system ensures that every shot is a masterpiece, allowing users to unleash their *creativity and express themselves through photography.*

Front-Facing Camera (Selfie Camera)

The Honor Magic V2 features a sophisticated front-facing camera, also known as the selfie camera, that delivers exceptional selfie photography and video calling capabilities. In this section, we'll explore the specifications, features, and functionalities of the front-facing camera on the Honor Magic V2.

1. Megapixels and Sensor

The front-facing camera of the Honor Magic V2 typically boasts a high-resolution sensor that captures sharp and detailed selfies. While the megapixel count may vary depending on the specific model and configuration of the device, it commonly ranges from 16MP to 32MP, ensuring crisp and clear selfies with ample detail and vibrancy. The high-resolution sensor of the front-facing camera allows users to capture stunning self-portraits and group selfies with ease.

2. Wide-Angle Lens and Field of View

The front-facing camera of the Honor Magic V2 is often equipped with a wide-angle lens that offers a generous field of view for capturing expansive selfies and group shots. The wide-angle lens ensures that users can fit more subjects into the frame, making it ideal for group selfies, scenic selfies, and capturing moments with friends and family. With a wider field of view, users can express *themselves creatively and capture more of their surroundings in their selfies.*

3. Beautification and AI Enhancement

The front-facing camera of the Honor Magic V2 includes built-in beautification features and AI enhancements that help users look their best in selfies. These features may include:

- *Beauty Mode: Beauty Mode applies real-time skin smoothing, blemish removal, and facial enhancements to selfies, helping users achieve flawless and radiant-looking skin in every shot. Users can adjust the level of beautification to suit their preferences and ensure that their selfies reflect their unique style and personality.*

- *AI Portrait Mode: AI Portrait Mode on the front-facing camera creates stunning portrait selfies by applying a natural bokeh effect to the background, blurring distractions and highlighting the subject. The camera system uses advanced AI algorithms to accurately detect and separate the subject from the background, ensuring that selfies are beautifully rendered with professional-looking bokeh effects.*

4. Selfie Lighting Effects

The Honor Magic V2's front-facing camera may feature built-in selfie lighting effects that allow users to enhance their selfies with creative lighting styles and effects. These lighting effects simulate studio lighting conditions, such as soft light, stage light, and butterfly light, to add drama, depth, and character to selfies. Users can choose from a variety of lighting effects to achieve the desired mood and atmosphere in their selfies, whether they're going for a natural look or a glamorous style.

The front-facing camera of the Honor Magic V2 offers a sophisticated selfie photography experience that empowers users to capture stunning self-portraits and group selfies with ease. With a high-resolution sensor, wide-angle lens, beautification features, AI enhancements, and selfie lighting effects, the front-facing camera ensures that every selfie is a masterpiece, allowing users to express themselves creatively and confidently in their photos.

Camera Software Features and Modes

The Honor Magic V2 comes with a comprehensive suite of camera software features and modes that enhance the photography and videography experience, providing users with creative tools and functionalities to capture stunning images and videos. In this section, we'll explore the various camera software features and modes available on the Honor Magic V2.

1. Pro Mode

Pro Mode on the Honor Magic V2 gives users manual control over various camera settings, allowing them to adjust parameters such as ISO, shutter speed, white balance, exposure compensation, and focus manually. Pro Mode is ideal for advanced users and photography enthusiasts who want precise control over their camera settings to achieve their desired photographic effects and creative vision.

2. AI Photography

The Honor Magic V2 features AI-powered photography capabilities that intelligently analyze scenes and subjects in real-time to optimize camera settings and enhance image quality. AI Photography automatically detects and adjusts camera settings for different scenes, subjects, and lighting conditions, ensuring that users can capture stunning photos with minimal effort. Whether it's landscapes, portraits, food, pets, or night scenes, AI Photography ensures that every shot is perfectly tailored to the environment and context.

3. Panorama Mode

Panorama Mode on the Honor Magic V2 allows users to capture sweeping panoramic images by stitching together multiple photos into a single wide-angle panorama. Users can pan the camera horizontally or vertically to capture expansive landscapes, cityscapes, or scenic vistas with stunning detail and perspective. Panorama Mode provides a creative and immersive way to capture the beauty of wide-open spaces and breathtaking landscapes.

4. HDR (High Dynamic Range)

HDR (High Dynamic Range) mode on the Honor Magic V2 enhances image quality by combining multiple exposures to capture a wider range of tones and details in high-contrast scenes. HDR mode preserves details in both highlights and shadows, ensuring that photos are well-exposed and balanced even in challenging lighting conditions. Whether it's bright skies, deep shadows, or backlit subjects, HDR mode ensures that users can capture true-to-life images with vibrant colors and rich detail.

5. Time-Lapse and Slow Motion

The Honor Magic V2 offers Time-Lapse and Slow Motion modes that allow users to create dynamic and cinematic videos with ease. Time-Lapse mode compresses long periods of time into short, accelerated videos, capturing the passage of time in creative and visually engaging ways. Slow Motion mode, on the other hand, records videos at a higher frame rate, allowing users to capture and replay fast-moving action with dramatic effect.

6. AR Stickers and Effects

The Honor Magic V2 features AR (Augmented Reality) stickers and effects that add fun and creativity to photos and videos. Users can choose from a variety of virtual stickers, filters, animations, and effects to overlay on their photos and videos, transforming ordinary moments into playful and imaginative creations. AR stickers and effects provide users with endless opportunities for self-expression and storytelling, allowing them to personalize their photos and videos with their unique style and personality.

The camera software features and modes on the Honor Magic V2 offer a wealth of creative tools and functionalities that empower users to capture stunning images and videos with ease. Whether it's manual controls in Pro Mode, AI-powered photography, panoramic *landscapes, HDR images, Time-Lapse videos, Slow Motion footage, or AR stickers and effects, the camera software on the Honor Magic V2 ensures that users can unleash their creativity and capture every moment with precision and style.*

Chapter Eight: Connectivity Options

Network Connectivity (5G, 4G, Wi-Fi)

The Honor Magic V2 offers a comprehensive range of network connectivity options, ensuring that users stay connected and productive wherever they go. From lightning-fast 5G connectivity to reliable 4G LTE and high-speed Wi-Fi, the Honor Magic V2 provides seamless access to the internet and online services. Let's explore the network connectivity options available on the Honor Magic V2 in more detail:

1. 5G Connectivity

The Honor Magic V2 supports 5G connectivity, the latest generation of mobile network technology that delivers *unprecedented speed, reliability, and responsiveness. With 5G, users can enjoy blazing-fast download and upload speeds, low latency, and enhanced network capacity, enabling them to stream high-definition videos, download large files, and access cloud-based services with ease. 5G connectivity transforms the way users experience mobile internet, unlocking new possibilities for communication, entertainment, and productivity.*

2. 4G LTE Connectivity

In addition to 5G, the Honor Magic V2 is compatible with 4G LTE networks, providing users with reliable and high-speed connectivity in areas where 5G coverage may not be available. 4G LTE offers fast download and upload speeds, low latency, and widespread coverage, ensuring that users can stay connected and productive even in remote or rural areas. Whether it's streaming videos, browsing the web, or video conferencing, 4G LTE connectivity ensures a smooth and seamless online experience.

3. Wi-Fi Connectivity

The Honor Magic V2 features dual-band Wi-Fi connectivity, allowing users to connect to both 2.4GHz and 5GHz Wi-Fi networks for optimal performance and reliability. Wi-Fi connectivity provides users with high-speed internet access in homes, offices, public spaces, and Wi-Fi hotspots, enabling them to browse the web, stream media, and download content without relying on mobile data. With support for the latest Wi-Fi standards such as Wi-Fi 6 (802.11ax), the

Honor Magic V2 ensures fast and stable connections for all Wi-Fi-enabled devices.

4. Connectivity Features

In addition to network connectivity, the Honor Magic V2 offers a range of connectivity features and technologies that enhance the user experience:

- Bluetooth: The Honor Magic V2 supports Bluetooth connectivity for wireless audio streaming, file sharing, and device pairing. Bluetooth enables users to connect their device to a wide range of Bluetooth-enabled accessories, such as headphones, speakers, keyboards, and smartwatches, for added convenience and versatility.
- NFC (Near Field Communication): Some models of the Honor Magic V2

may include NFC capabilities, allowing users to make contactless payments, transfer files, and access NFC-enabled services with ease. NFC enables seamless communication between devices and facilitates convenient interactions in various scenarios, such as mobile payments, transit ticketing, and electronic access control.

The Honor Magic V2 offers a comprehensive range of network connectivity options, including 5G, 4G LTE, and Wi-Fi, ensuring that users stay connected and productive wherever they go. With lightning-fast 5G connectivity, reliable 4G LTE coverage, and high-speed Wi-Fi connectivity, the Honor Magic V2 provides seamless access to the internet and online services, enabling users to stay connected, entertained, and productive on the go.

Bluetooth and NFC

The Honor Magic V2 comes equipped with Bluetooth and NFC capabilities, providing users with versatile connectivity options for wireless communication, data transfer, and contactless interactions. In this section, we'll explore the functionalities and benefits of Bluetooth and NFC on the Honor Magic V2.

1. Bluetooth Connectivity

Bluetooth technology enables wireless communication between devices over short distances, making it ideal for connecting smartphones, tablets, computers, and a wide range of accessories and peripherals. The

Honor Magic V2 features Bluetooth connectivity, allowing users to:

- *Wireless Audio Streaming: Users can pair their Honor Magic V2 with Bluetooth-enabled headphones, earbuds, speakers, and car audio systems for wireless audio streaming. Bluetooth audio streaming provides freedom of movement and eliminates the need for cumbersome cables, allowing users to enjoy their favorite music, podcasts, and audiobooks on the go.*

- *File Sharing: Bluetooth enables users to transfer files, photos, videos, and documents between their Honor Magic V2 and other Bluetooth-enabled devices, such as smartphones, tablets, and laptops. Bluetooth file sharing provides a convenient and wireless method for sharing content with friends, family, and colleagues without relying on internet connectivity or data cables.*

- *Device Pairing: Bluetooth allows users to pair their Honor Magic V2 with a wide range of Bluetooth-enabled accessories and peripherals, such as keyboards, mice, game controllers, smartwatches, fitness trackers, and more. Device pairing enables seamless integration and interaction between devices, enhancing productivity, convenience, and versatility.*

2. NFC (Near Field Communication)

NFC is a short-range wireless communication technology that enables contactless interactions between devices, tags, and NFC-enabled objects. The Honor Magic V2 features NFC capabilities, allowing users to:

- *Contactless Payments:* With NFC, users can make secure and convenient contactless payments using their Honor Magic V2 at NFC-enabled payment terminals. Supported payment methods, such as Google Pay or Huawei Pay, allow users to add their credit or debit cards to their device and tap to pay at participating merchants, eliminating the need to carry physical cards or cash.

- *File Transfer:* NFC enables users to transfer files, photos, videos, and contacts between their Honor Magic V2 and other NFC-enabled devices by simply tapping them together. NFC file transfer provides a quick and easy method for sharing content between devices without the need for Wi-Fi, Bluetooth, or data cables.

- *Smart Interactions:* NFC tags and stickers can be programmed to trigger specific actions or functions when tapped with an NFC-enabled device like the Honor Magic V2. Users can create personalized NFC tags for tasks such as setting alarms, adjusting device settings, launching apps, or sharing Wi-Fi network credentials, streamlining everyday tasks and routines.

Bluetooth and NFC capabilities on the Honor Magic V2 provide users with versatile connectivity options for wireless communication, data transfer, and contactless interactions. *Whether it's streaming audio, sharing files, pairing accessories, making contactless payments, or automating tasks with NFC tags, Bluetooth and NFC empower users to stay connected, productive, and efficient in various scenarios and use cases.*

GPS and Navigation Features

The Honor Magic V2 is equipped with advanced GPS (Global Positioning System) technology and navigation features that provide users with accurate location information, turn-by-turn directions, and real-time navigation assistance. In this section, we'll explore the functionalities and benefits of GPS and navigation features on the Honor Magic V2.

1. GPS Technology

GPS is a satellite-based navigation system that enables devices like the Honor Magic V2 to determine their precise location, speed, and elevation anywhere on Earth. The Honor Magic V2 utilizes GPS technology to provide users with accurate location data for various applications and services, including mapping, navigation, fitness tracking, and location-based services. With GPS, users can:

- *Navigate: GPS enables users to navigate to their desired destinations with confidence by providing turn-by-turn directions, real-time traffic updates, and estimated arrival times. Whether it's driving, walking, cycling, or using public transportation, GPS navigation ensures that users can* reach their destinations efficiently and safely.

- *Explore: GPS allows users to explore new places, discover points of interest, and find nearby attractions, restaurants, shops, and landmarks with ease. Whether it's exploring a new city, hiking in the wilderness, or traveling to unfamiliar destinations, GPS helps users navigate and explore their surroundings with confidence and convenience.*

- *Track: GPS enables users to track their activities, routes, and workouts with precision, allowing them to monitor their progress, performance, and fitness goals. Whether it's running, cycling, hiking, or skiing, GPS tracking provides valuable insights into users' activities, including distance traveled, pace, elevation gain, and calories burned.*

2. Navigation Features

In addition to basic GPS functionality, the Honor Magic V2 offers a range of navigation features and services that enhance the user experience:

- *Voice-Guided Navigation: The Honor Magic V2 provides voice-guided navigation instructions that guide users to their destinations with spoken turn-by-turn directions. Voice-guided navigation ensures that users can keep their eyes on the road and hands on the wheel while driving, cycling, or walking, minimizing distractions and enhancing safety.*

- *Real-Time Traffic Updates: The Honor Magic V2 offers real-time traffic updates and incident reports that help users avoid traffic congestion, accidents, road closures, and other delays during their journeys. Real-time traffic updates provide alternative routes and detours to minimize travel time and ensure smooth and efficient navigation.*

- *Offline Maps: The Honor Magic V2 supports offline maps, allowing users to download maps of specific regions or areas for offline use. Offline maps enable users to navigate and explore without relying on a cellular or Wi-Fi connection, making them ideal for traveling in remote or international* destinations where internet access may be limited or unavailable.

GPS and navigation features on the Honor Magic V2 provide users with accurate location information, turn-by-turn directions, and real-time navigation assistance for various activities and scenarios. Whether it's navigating to destinations, exploring new places, tracking activities, or avoiding traffic congestion, GPS and navigation features ensure that users can travel with confidence and convenience, wherever their adventures take them.

Chapter Nine: Audio and Multimedia

Speaker Quality and Placement

The Honor Magic V2 is designed to deliver immersive audio experiences with its high-quality speakers strategically placed for optimal sound projection and clarity. In this section, we'll explore the speaker quality and placement on the Honor Magic V2.

1. Speaker Configuration

The Honor Magic V2 typically features a stereo speaker setup, with speakers positioned at the top and bottom or on the front-facing bezels of the device. This stereo configuration enables the Honor Magic V2 to deliver rich, balanced sound with enhanced stereo separation and spatial imaging, making it ideal for multimedia consumption, gaming, and hands-free calling.

2. Sound Quality

The speakers on the Honor Magic V2 are engineered to produce clear, crisp audio with robust bass, detailed midrange, and sparkling highs. Whether you're watching videos, listening to music, or playing games, the Honor Magic V2's speakers deliver immersive sound that enhances the overall multimedia experience. The high-quality sound output ensures that users can enjoy their favorite content with fidelity and immersion, whether they're watching movies, streaming music, or playing games.

3. Placement and Directionality

The placement of the speakers on the Honor Magic V2 is carefully optimized to deliver optimal sound projection and directionality. By positioning the speakers strategically, the Honor Magic V2 ensures that sound is directed towards the user for maximum clarity and immersion. Whether you're holding the device in landscape or portrait orientation, the speakers deliver consistent and immersive sound that fills the room and enhances the multimedia experience.

4. Dolby Atmos Support

Some models of the Honor Magic V2 may feature Dolby Atmos support, a powerful audio technology that enhances sound quality and spatial realism for an immersive listening experience. Dolby Atmos creates a three-dimensional audio environment that surrounds the listener with lifelike sound, making movies, music, and games come alive with depth, detail, and dimensionality. With Dolby Atmos support, the Honor Magic V2 delivers a truly cinematic audio experience that transports users into the heart of the action.

The Honor Magic V2 offers high-quality speakers strategically placed for optimal sound projection and clarity, delivering immersive audio experiences for multimedia consumption, gaming, and hands-free calling. With its stereo speaker configuration, clear sound quality, precise placement, and optional Dolby Atmos support, the Honor Magic V2 ensures that users can enjoy their favorite content with fidelity and immersion, whether they're watching movies, streaming music, or playing games.

Audio Enhancements

The Honor Magic V2 is equipped with advanced audio enhancements that elevate the audio experience, delivering immersive sound quality and spatial realism for multimedia consumption, gaming, and hands-free calling. In this section, we'll explore the audio enhancements available on the Honor Magic V2.

1. Dolby Atmos

Dolby Atmos is a powerful audio technology that creates a three-dimensional soundstage, surrounding the listener with lifelike audio that moves in all directions. The Honor Magic V2 may feature Dolby Atmos support, enhancing sound quality and spatial realism for an immersive listening experience. Dolby Atmos optimizes audio content by dynamically adjusting volume, equalization, and spatial positioning to match the device's capabilities and the listener's environment. Whether you're watching movies, streaming music, or playing games, Dolby Atmos ensures that you're fully immersed in the audio experience, with rich, detailed sound that transports you into the heart of the action.

2. Equalizer Settings

The Honor Magic V2 may offer customizable equalizer settings that allow users to fine-tune audio playback according to their preferences and listening environment. Equalizer settings enable users to adjust the balance of bass, midrange, and treble frequencies to optimize sound quality and clarity. Whether you prefer punchy bass for music playback, clear vocals for video watching, or balanced audio for gaming, the customizable equalizer settings on the Honor Magic V2 ensure that you can tailor the audio experience to suit your tastes and preferences.

3. Audio Profiles

Some models of the Honor Magic V2 may include audio profiles or presets that optimize sound quality for different types of content or listening scenarios. Audio profiles automatically adjust audio settings, such as volume, equalization, and spatialization, to enhance the audio experience for specific use cases, such as music playback, movie watching, gaming, or hands-free calling. With audio profiles, users can enjoy optimized sound quality and immersion for *their favorite content, without the need for manual adjustment.*

4. Audio Enhancement Technologies

In addition to Dolby Atmos, the Honor Magic V2 may incorporate other audio enhancement technologies and algorithms that improve sound quality and clarity. These technologies may include:

- *Virtual Surround Sound: Virtual surround sound technology simulates the immersive audio experience of a multi-speaker surround sound system, creating the illusion of audio coming from multiple directions. Virtual surround sound enhances spatial realism and immersion for movies, games, and virtual reality experiences, allowing users to feel like they're in the center of the action.*

- *Noise Cancellation: Noise cancellation technology suppresses background noise and interference during audio playback and hands-free calling, ensuring clear and intelligible communication even in noisy environments. Noise cancellation enhances the clarity of audio recordings, voice calls, and video chats, allowing users to communicate effectively without distractions or interruptions.*

The Honor Magic V2 offers advanced audio enhancements that elevate the audio experience, delivering immersive sound quality and spatial realism for multimedia consumption, gaming, and hands-free calling. Whether it's Dolby Atmos support, customizable equalizer settings, audio profiles, or other audio enhancement technologies, the Honor Magic V2 ensures that users can enjoy their favorite content with clarity, depth, and immersion, regardless of the listening environment or use case.

Multimedia Playback Capabilities

The Honor Magic V2 offers versatile multimedia playback capabilities, allowing users to enjoy a wide range of audio and video content with clarity, fidelity, and immersion. In this section, we'll explore the multimedia playback capabilities of the Honor Magic V2.

1. Audio Playback

The Honor Magic V2 supports various audio formats and codecs, ensuring compatibility with a wide range of music files and streaming services. Whether you're listening to your favorite albums, podcasts, or audiobooks, the Honor Magic V2 delivers rich, detailed sound with immersive audio enhancements. With support for high-resolution audio formats, customizable equalizer settings, and optional Dolby Atmos support, the Honor Magic V2 ensures that users can enjoy their favorite music with fidelity and immersion, whether they're using headphones, external speakers, or the device's built-in speakers.

2. Video Playback

The Honor Magic V2 offers seamless video playback capabilities, allowing users to enjoy high-definition video content with vibrant colors, sharp detail, and smooth playback. Whether you're streaming movies, watching videos, or playing games, the Honor Magic V2 delivers stunning visuals and immersive audio to enhance the viewing experience. With support for popular video formats and codecs, as well as advanced display technologies such as OLED or AMOLED screens, HDR support, and high refresh rates, the Honor Magic V2 ensures that users can enjoy their favorite video content with cinematic quality and realism.

3. Streaming Services

The Honor Magic V2 provides access to a wide range of streaming services for multimedia consumption, including music streaming services such as Spotify, Apple

Music, and YouTube Music, as well as video streaming services such as Netflix, Amazon Prime Video, and YouTube. Whether you're streaming music, movies, TV shows, or live events, the Honor Magic V2 ensures seamless access to your favorite content, with high-quality audio and video playback that enhances the overall streaming experience. With support for high-speed internet connectivity options such as 5G, 4G LTE, and Wi-Fi, the Honor Magic V2 ensures smooth and uninterrupted streaming, even in high-definition or 4K resolution.

4. Gaming and Entertainment

The Honor Magic V2 offers immersive gaming and entertainment experiences, with advanced audio and visual technologies that bring games and multimedia content to life.

Whether you're playing mobile games, watching streaming videos, or browsing social media, the Honor Magic V2 delivers smooth performance, vibrant graphics, and immersive sound that enhance the overall gaming and entertainment experience. With support for high-refresh-rate displays, responsive touch controls, and powerful processors, the Honor Magic V2 ensures that users can enjoy their favorite games and multimedia content with fluidity, realism, and immersion.

The Honor Magic V2 offers versatile multimedia playback capabilities that enhance the audio and video experience, allowing users to enjoy a wide range of content with clarity, fidelity, and immersion. Whether it's music playback, video streaming, gaming, or entertainment, the

Honor Magic V2 ensures seamless access to your favorite content, with high-quality audio and video playback that brings content to life. With advanced audio enhancements, support for popular streaming services, and immersive gaming and entertainment features, the Honor Magic V2 delivers an unparalleled multimedia experience that elevates the way users consume and enjoy content on their device.

Chapter Ten: Security Features

Biometric Security

The Honor Magic V2 prioritizes user security with advanced biometric authentication technologies, including fingerprint scanning and facial recognition. These features provide users with convenient and secure methods to unlock their device, authenticate transactions, and protect sensitive information. In this section, we'll explore the biometric security features of the Honor Magic V2.

1. Fingerprint Scanner

The Honor Magic V2 features a fingerprint scanner, typically located on the device's display or rear panel, that enables users to unlock their device and authenticate transactions with a simple touch of their finger. The fingerprint scanner on the Honor Magic V2 utilizes advanced biometric technology to accurately and securely recognize unique fingerprint patterns, ensuring fast and reliable authentication. Users can register multiple fingerprints for added convenience and flexibility, allowing them to unlock their device from various angles or positions. With its fast and accurate fingerprint scanning capabilities, the Honor Magic V2 provides users with a seamless and secure way to access their device and protect their personal information.

2. Facial Recognition

In addition to fingerprint scanning, the Honor Magic V2 may offer facial recognition technology that allows users to unlock their device simply by looking at it. Facial recognition on the Honor Magic V2 utilizes advanced algorithms and sensors to analyze facial features and patterns, creating a unique biometric profile for each user. Users can register their face with the device's facial recognition system, which then securely stores and verifies their facial data during the authentication process. With its intuitive and secure facial recognition technology, the Honor Magic V2 provides users with a convenient and hands-free way to unlock their device and access their apps, photos, and other sensitive information.

3. Security and Privacy

Both fingerprint scanning and facial recognition on the Honor Magic V2 are designed with security and privacy in mind, ensuring that user biometric data is protected and encrypted to prevent unauthorized access or misuse. Biometric data is securely stored on the device and never transmitted over the internet or stored in the cloud, minimizing the risk of data breaches or identity theft. Additionally, users have full control over their biometric authentication settings, allowing them to enable or disable fingerprint scanning and facial recognition as desired. With its robust biometric security features, the Honor Magic V2 provides users with peace of mind knowing that their device and personal information are protected by advanced biometric authentication technologies.

The Honor Magic V2 offers advanced biometric security features, including fingerprint scanning and facial recognition, that provide users with convenient and secure methods to unlock their device and protect their personal information. With its fast and accurate fingerprint scanner and intuitive facial recognition technology, the Honor Magic V2 ensures that users can access their device quickly and securely, without compromising on privacy or security. Whether it's unlocking the device, authenticating transactions, or protecting sensitive information, the biometric security features of the Honor Magic V2 provide users with peace of mind knowing that their device and personal data are protected by advanced biometric authentication technologies.

Privacy Features and Settings

The Honor Magic V2 prioritizes user privacy with a suite of advanced features and settings designed to safeguard personal data and protect user privacy. In this section, we'll explore the privacy features and settings available on the Honor Magic V2.

1. App Permissions

The Honor Magic V2 allows users to manage app permissions, giving them control over which apps have access to sensitive data such as location, contacts, camera, microphone, and storage. Users can review and customize app permissions for each installed app, granting or revoking access to specific permissions based on their preferences and privacy concerns. With granular control over app permissions, users can ensure that their personal data remains secure and protected from unauthorized access or misuse.

2. Privacy Dashboard

The Honor Magic V2 may feature a privacy dashboard that provides users with an overview of their app permissions, privacy settings, and data usage. The privacy dashboard allows users to monitor which apps have access to sensitive data and how that data is being used, empowering them to make informed decisions about their privacy and security. Users can review app permissions, app usage statistics, and privacy recommendations to ensure that their personal data is protected and their privacy preferences are respected.

3. Secure Folder

Some models of the Honor Magic V2 may include a secure folder feature that allows users to create a private and encrypted space on their device to store sensitive files, photos, videos, and apps. The secure folder is protected by a separate password, PIN, or biometric authentication method, ensuring that only authorized users can access its contents. With the secure folder, users can keep their personal data secure and private, even if their device is lost, stolen, or accessed by unauthorized individuals.

4. Private Browsing Mode

The Honor Magic V2 may offer a private browsing mode that allows users to browse the internet without saving browsing history, cookies, or other browsing data. Private browsing mode prevents websites from tracking users' online activities and ensures that their browsing history remains private and confidential. Whether it's shopping for gifts, banking online, or accessing sensitive *websites, private browsing mode provides users with a secure and anonymous browsing experience that protects their privacy and security.*

The Honor Magic V2 offers advanced privacy features and settings that empower users to take control of their personal data and protect their privacy in an increasingly connected world. From managing app permissions and monitoring data usage to creating secure folders and browsing the internet anonymously, the privacy features and settings of the Honor Magic V2 ensure that users can safeguard their personal information and maintain their privacy and security with confidence.

Device Encryption and Protection

The Honor Magic V2 prioritizes the security of user data with robust device encryption and protection mechanisms that safeguard sensitive information from unauthorized access and misuse. In this section, we'll explore the device encryption and protection features available on the Honor Magic V2.

1. Data Encryption

The Honor Magic V2 employs data encryption to protect user data stored on the device from unauthorized access or interception. Data encryption uses cryptographic algorithms to encode user data, making it unreadable to anyone who does not have the encryption key. This ensures that even if the device is lost, stolen, or accessed by unauthorized individuals, user data remains secure and protected from prying eyes. The Honor Magic V2 encrypts data at rest, including files, photos, videos, app data, and system files, ensuring comprehensive protection for all user data stored on the device.

2. Secure Boot

The Honor Magic V2 features secure boot technology that protects the device's operating system and firmware from tampering or unauthorized modifications. Secure boot verifies the integrity of the device's boot process and ensures that only trusted and authenticated software components are loaded during startup. This prevents malicious software or unauthorized modifications from compromising the security and stability of the device, ensuring that users can trust the integrity of their device's operating system and firmware.

3. Device Lock Screen

The Honor Magic V2 offers a variety of device lock screen options to secure access to the device and protect user data from unauthorized access. Users can choose from various lock screen methods, including PIN, password, pattern, fingerprint scanning, and facial recognition, depending on their preferences and security needs. With a secure lock screen in place, users can prevent unauthorized users from accessing their device or sensitive information, ensuring that their data remains protected at all times.

4. Find My Device

The Honor Magic V2 may include a Find My Device feature that allows users to locate, lock, or remotely wipe their device in case it is lost or stolen. Find My Device uses GPS and internet connectivity to pinpoint the location of the device on a map, enabling users to track its whereabouts in real-time. In addition to location tracking, Find My Device allows users to remotely lock the device with a custom message and contact information, preventing unauthorized access to user data. Users can also remotely wipe their device to erase all data stored on it, ensuring that sensitive information remains protected from unauthorized access or misuse.

The Honor Magic V2 offers robust device encryption and protection mechanisms that safeguard user data and ensure the security and integrity of the device. From data encryption and secure boot to device lock screen options and Find My Device functionality, the Honor Magic V2 provides comprehensive protection for user data and privacy. With these advanced security features in place, users can trust that their sensitive information remains secure and protected from unauthorized access or misuse, providing peace of mind and confidence in their digital interactions and activities.

Chapter Eleven: User Tips and Tricks

Compatible Accessories

The Honor Magic V2 offers a range of compatible accessories that enhance the functionality, protection, and style of the device. From cases and screen protectors to chargers and headphones, these accessories are designed to complement the Honor Magic V2 and provide users with added convenience and customization options. In this section, we'll explore some of the compatible accessories available for the Honor Magic V2.

1. Cases and Covers

Protective cases and covers are essential accessories for safeguarding the Honor Magic V2 against drops, bumps, scratches, and other daily wear and tear. Compatible cases and covers are available in a variety of materials, styles, and colors to suit different preferences and lifestyles. Whether you prefer slim and lightweight cases for minimalistic protection or rugged and heavy-duty cases for maximum durability, there are plenty of options to choose from to keep your Honor Magic V2 safe and secure.

2. Screen Protectors

Screen protectors are another essential accessory for preserving the pristine condition of the Honor Magic V2's display and preventing scratches, smudges, and fingerprints. Compatible screen protectors are available in various materials, including tempered glass and film, with different levels of thickness and hardness to provide optimal protection without sacrificing touchscreen sensitivity or display clarity. Whether you prefer clear or matte finishes, there are screen protectors available to suit your preferences and protect your Honor Magic V2's display from damage.

3. Chargers and Power Banks

Chargers and power banks are essential accessories for keeping the Honor Magic V2 powered up and ready to go throughout the day. Compatible chargers and power banks come in various configurations, including wired and wireless options, fast charging capabilities, and portable designs for on-the-go convenience. Whether you need a spare charger for home or office use or a power bank for travel or outdoor adventures, there are plenty of options available to ensure that your Honor Magic V2 stays charged and ready for action whenever you need it.

4. Headphones and Earbuds

Headphones and earbuds are popular accessories for enjoying music, podcasts, videos, and games on the Honor Magic V2 with immersive sound quality and clarity. Compatible headphones and earbuds come in various styles and designs, including wired and wireless options, in-ear and over-ear styles, and noise-canceling features for optimal audio performance and comfort. Whether you prefer premium audio quality for music listening or hands-free convenience for calls and voice commands, there are headphones and earbuds available to suit your preferences and enhance your multimedia experience on the Honor Magic V2.

The Honor Magic V2 offers a wide range of compatible accessories that enhance the functionality, protection, and style of the device. From cases and screen protectors to chargers and headphones, these accessories provide users with added convenience, customization options, and peace of mind. Whether you're looking to protect your device, extend its battery life, or enhance your multimedia experience, there are plenty of compatible accessories available to complement your Honor Magic V2 and tailor it to your needs and preferences.

Optional Peripherals

In addition to essential accessories like cases, chargers, and headphones, the Honor Magic V2 offers optional peripherals that enhance productivity, creativity, and entertainment on the device. From styluses and game controllers to docking stations and external monitors, these peripherals expand the capabilities of the Honor Magic V2 and provide users with new ways to interact with their device. In this section, we'll explore some of the optional peripherals available for the Honor Magic V2.

1. Stylus Pen

A stylus pen is a versatile accessory that allows users to interact with the Honor Magic V2's touchscreen with precision and control, making it ideal for note-taking, drawing, sketching, and digital artwork. Compatible stylus pens feature pressure sensitivity, tilt recognition, and customizable buttons for a natural and intuitive writing and drawing experience. Whether you're a student taking notes in class, an artist creating digital illustrations, or a professional annotating documents, a stylus pen provides added versatility and creativity to your Honor Magic V2.

2. Game Controllers

Game controllers are essential accessories for gamers who want a more immersive and tactile gaming experience on the Honor Magic V2. Compatible game controllers come in various configurations, including wireless and wired options, ergonomic designs, and customizable buttons for optimal control and comfort. *Whether you're playing action-packed shooters, thrilling racing games, or immersive RPGs, a game controller enhances gameplay responsiveness and precision, allowing you to enjoy your favorite games to the fullest on the Honor Magic V2.*

3. Docking Stations

Docking stations are convenient accessories that allow users to connect the Honor Magic V2 to external displays, keyboards, mice, and other peripherals for enhanced productivity and multitasking. Compatible docking stations feature multiple ports, including HDMI, USB-C, and Ethernet, for seamless connectivity and expansion options. Whether you're working on a presentation, editing documents, or streaming media, a docking station transforms the Honor Magic V2 into a versatile desktop workstation, allowing you to maximize your productivity and efficiency.

4. External Monitors

External monitors are essential accessories for users who need additional screen real estate for multitasking, content creation, and entertainment on the Honor Magic V2. Compatible external monitors come in various sizes, resolutions, and configurations, including ultrawide and curved displays, for immersive viewing experiences and enhanced productivity. Whether you're editing videos, coding software, or watching movies, an external monitor expands your workspace and enhances your multimedia experience on the Honor Magic V2, allowing you to see more and do more with your device.

The Honor Magic V2 offers optional peripherals that enhance productivity, creativity, and entertainment on the device, including stylus pens, game controllers, docking stations, and external monitors. Whether you're taking notes, playing games, or working on a presentation, these peripherals expand the capabilities of the Honor Magic V2 and provide users with new ways to interact with their device. With versatile connectivity options and compatibility with a wide range of peripherals, the Honor Magic V2 ensures that users can tailor their device to suit their needs and preferences, enhancing their overall experience and productivity.

Chapter Twelve: User Tips and Tricks

Hidden Features and Shortcuts

The Honor Magic V2 is packed with a plethora of features and shortcuts that can enhance user experience and productivity. While many of these features are easily accessible through the device's user interface, there are some hidden gems that users may not be aware of. In this section, we'll explore some of the hidden features and shortcuts of the Honor Magic V2 that can help users make the most out of their device.

1. Quick Settings Customization

Did you know that you can customize the Quick Settings panel on your Honor Magic V2 to include your most frequently used settings and shortcuts? Simply swipe down from the top of the screen to access the Quick Settings panel, then tap the edit icon or long-press on any tile to rearrange or add new tiles. You can add shortcuts for Wi-Fi, Bluetooth, flashlight, screen brightness, and more, allowing you to access your favorite settings with just a few taps.

2. One-Handed Mode

If you're finding it difficult to use your Honor Magic V2 with one hand, you can enable the one-handed mode for easier navigation and operation. Simply swipe down from the bottom of the screen with your thumb to activate one-handed mode, which reduces the size of the screen and moves it closer to your thumb for easier reachability. You can adjust the size and position of the one-handed mode screen to suit your preferences and make it more comfortable to use your device with one hand.

3. Gesture Navigation

Gesture navigation allows you to navigate your Honor Magic V2 with intuitive gestures, eliminating the need for on-screen navigation buttons. You can swipe up from the bottom of the screen to go home, swipe up and hold for recent apps, or swipe from the left or right edge of the screen to go back. Gesture navigation provides a more immersive and seamless user experience, allowing you to maximize the screen real estate and focus on the content without distractions.

4. Smart Screen Rotation

Tired of your screen rotating every time you tilt your device slightly? The Honor Magic V2 features smart screen rotation technology that uses the device's sensors to detect the orientation of your face and adjust the screen rotation accordingly. This means that your screen will only rotate when you want it to, based on the position of your face relative to the device. Smart screen rotation ensures that you can enjoy your content without interruptions, even if you're lying down or holding your device at an angle.

5. Scheduled Power On/Off

Need your Honor Magic V2 to power on or off at specific times of the day? You can use the scheduled power on/off feature to automatically turn your device on or off according to your predefined schedule.

Simply go to Settings > Smart Assistance > Scheduled power on/off and set the desired power on and off times. This feature is particularly useful for conserving battery life overnight or ensuring that your device is ready to go when you wake up in the morning.

The Honor Magic V2 is equipped with a variety of hidden features and shortcuts that can enhance user experience and productivity. From customizable Quick Settings to one-handed mode, gesture navigation, smart screen rotation, and scheduled power on/off, these hidden gems allow users to make the most out of their device and tailor it to their specific needs and preferences. By exploring and mastering these hidden features and shortcuts, users can unlock the full potential of their Honor

Magic V2 and enjoy a more seamless and intuitive user experience.

Optimization Tips for Better Performance and Battery Life

Maximizing the performance and battery life of your Honor Magic V2 is crucial for ensuring a smooth and efficient user experience. By following some optimization tips and best practices, you can enhance the performance of your device and prolong its battery life. In this section, we'll explore some optimization tips for getting the most out of your Honor Magic V2.

1. Manage Background Apps

Background apps can consume system resources and drain battery life, even when you're not actively using them. To optimize performance and battery life, it's essential to manage background apps effectively. You can manually close background apps by accessing the Recent Apps screen and swiping away unnecessary apps. Additionally, you can enable battery optimization settings to restrict background activity for specific apps, ensuring that they only run when necessary.

2. Optimize Display Settings

The display is one of the most power-hungry components of your Honor Magic V2. To conserve battery life, consider optimizing your display settings. You can reduce screen brightness, enable adaptive brightness to adjust brightness automatically based on ambient lighting conditions, and shorten the screen timeout duration to minimize the amount of time the display remains active when not in use. These adjustments can significantly reduce battery consumption without sacrificing visibility or usability.

3. Enable Power Saving Modes

The Honor Magic V2 offers built-in power-saving modes that can help extend battery life by limiting background activity, reducing performance, and optimizing system settings. You can enable power-saving modes manually when you need to conserve battery life, or set up automatic triggers based on battery level or usage patterns. Power-saving modes can disable features like GPS, Bluetooth, and sync services temporarily to minimize power consumption and maximize battery life when you're not actively using your device.

4. Update Software Regularly

Software updates often include performance optimizations, bug fixes, and security patches that can improve the overall performance and stability of your Honor Magic V2. It's essential to keep your device's software up to date by installing the latest updates from Honor as they become available. You can check for software updates manually by going to Settings > System > Software update and selecting Check for updates. By staying up to date with the latest software releases, you can ensure that your device operates efficiently and securely.

5. Monitor Battery Usage

Understanding how your device consumes battery power can help you identify and address potential issues that may be affecting performance and battery life. The Honor Magic V2 provides built-in battery usage statistics that allow you to monitor which apps and services are consuming the most battery power. You can access battery usage statistics by going to Settings > Battery > Battery usage. By identifying battery-hungry apps and adjusting their settings or usage patterns, you can optimize battery life and improve overall device performance.

Optimizing performance and battery life is essential for ensuring a smooth and efficient user experience on your Honor Magic V2. By managing background apps, optimizing display settings, enabling power-saving modes, updating software regularly, and monitoring battery usage, you can maximize the performance and longevity of your device. These optimization tips and best practices allow you to get the most out of your Honor Magic V2 and enjoy a seamless and reliable user experience for years to come.

Troubleshooting Common Issues

While the Honor Magic V2 is a reliable and feature-rich device, users may encounter occasional issues that can affect performance or usability. Fortunately, many common issues can be resolved with simple troubleshooting steps. In this section, we'll explore some common issues users may encounter with the Honor Magic V2 and how to troubleshoot them effectively.

1. Device Freezes or Becomes Unresponsive

If your Honor Magic V2 freezes or becomes unresponsive, try the following troubleshooting steps:

- Restart the device by holding down the power button for a few seconds until the power menu appears, then select Restart.
- If the device remains unresponsive, perform a force restart by holding down the power button and volume down button simultaneously for about 10 seconds until the device restarts.
- Check for and install any available software updates, as they may include bug fixes or performance improvements that address the issue.

2. Battery Drains Quickly

If you notice that your Honor Magic V2's battery drains quickly, try the following troubleshooting steps:

- *Check battery usage statistics in the device settings to identify apps or services consuming excessive battery power, then adjust their settings or usage patterns accordingly.*
- *Reduce screen brightness and enable power-saving modes to minimize battery consumption.*
- *Close background apps that are not in use to prevent them from draining battery power unnecessarily.*
- *If the battery continues to drain quickly, consider performing a factory reset to restore the device to its default settings and eliminate any software-related issues.*

3. Connectivity Issues

If you're experiencing connectivity issues with Wi-Fi, Bluetooth, or mobile data on your Honor Magic V2, try the following troubleshooting steps:

- *Toggle airplane mode on and off to reset network connections.*
- *Restart the device to refresh network settings.*
- *Forget and reconnect to Wi-Fi networks or Bluetooth devices to resolve connection issues.*
- *If the issue persists, check for and install any available software updates, as they may include fixes for connectivity issues.*

4. App Crashes or Error Messages

If you encounter app crashes or error messages on your Honor Magic V2, try the following troubleshooting steps:

- Force close the app by accessing the Recent Apps screen and swiping away the problematic app.
- Clear the app cache and data in the device settings to resolve any temporary issues.
- Check for and install any available updates for the app from the Google Play Store, as they may include bug fixes or stability improvements.
- If the issue persists, uninstall and reinstall the app to ensure a clean installation and resolve any corrupted files or settings.

Many common issues users may encounter with the Honor Magic V2 can be resolved with simple troubleshooting steps. By following the tips outlined in this section, you can effectively troubleshoot and resolve issues related to device freezes, battery drain, connectivity issues, and app crashes. If you're unable to resolve the issue on your own, consider reaching out to Honor customer support or seeking assistance from a professional technician for further assistance.

Chapter Thirteen: Conclusion

After exploring the Honor Magic V2 in-depth, it's clear that this device offers a compelling combination of performance, features, and innovation. Throughout this review and user guide, we've covered various aspects of the Honor Magic V2, from its design and display to its performance, camera system, and security features. Now, let's summarize the key points and share final thoughts on the Honor Magic V2.

Summary of Key Points

- *Design and Build Quality: The Honor Magic V2 features a sleek and modern design with premium build materials, offering a comfortable and ergonomic user experience.*

- *Display Technology: With its vibrant OLED display, the Honor Magic V2 delivers stunning visuals with rich colors and deep blacks, enhancing the overall viewing experience.*

- *Performance and Hardware: Powered by a high-performance processor and ample RAM, the Honor Magic V2 offers smooth and responsive performance for multitasking, gaming, and productivity.*

- *Camera System: The Honor Magic V2 boasts a versatile camera system with advanced features and modes, allowing users to capture stunning photos and videos in various lighting conditions.*

- *Security Features: Equipped with biometric security features, device encryption, and privacy settings, the*

Honor Magic V2 prioritizes user security and privacy.

- User Tips and Tricks: From hidden features and shortcuts to optimization tips and troubleshooting advice, users can maximize the performance and usability of their Honor Magic V2.

Final Thoughts on the Honor Magic V2

In conclusion, the Honor Magic V2 is a standout device that offers a premium user experience with its impressive performance, stunning display, versatile camera system, and robust security features. Whether you're a power user looking for top-of-the-line performance or a casual user seeking a reliable and feature-rich smartphone, the Honor Magic V2 delivers on all fronts. With its sleek design, innovative features, and *user-friendly interface, the Honor Magic V2 stands out as a compelling option in the competitive smartphone market.*

As technology continues to evolve, the Honor Magic V2 remains at the forefront of innovation, offering users a glimpse into the future of mobile devices. With its cutting-edge features, intuitive user experience, and exceptional value, the Honor Magic V2 sets a new standard for what a smartphone can be. Whether you're capturing memories, staying productive on the go, or simply staying connected with loved ones, the Honor Magic V2 is the perfect companion for all your mobile needs.

In summary, the Honor Magic V2 is more than just a smartphone—it's a testament to Honor's commitment to innovation, quality, and user satisfaction. With its blend of style, performance, and innovation, the Honor Magic V2 is sure to impress even the most discerning smartphone users.

Recommendation for Prospective Buyers

If you're considering purchasing the Honor Magic V2, here are some recommendations to help you make an informed decision:

1. Performance Seekers: If you prioritize performance and want a device that can handle demanding tasks with ease, the Honor Magic V2 is an excellent choice. With its powerful processor, ample RAM, and optimized software, the Honor Magic V2 delivers smooth and responsive performance for multitasking, gaming, and productivity.

2. Photography Enthusiasts: If photography is a priority for you, the Honor Magic V2's versatile camera system won't disappoint. With its advanced camera features and modes, including AI enhancements and night mode, the Honor Magic V2 allows you to capture stunning photos and videos in any situation.

3. Security-Conscious Users: If security and privacy are top concerns for you, the Honor Magic V2 offers a range of advanced security features to keep your data safe and secure. From biometric authentication methods to device encryption and privacy settings, the Honor Magic V2 prioritizes user security and privacy.

4. Multimedia Enthusiasts: If you enjoy streaming videos, listening to music, or playing games on your smartphone, the Honor Magic V2's vibrant OLED display and immersive audio capabilities make it an excellent choice. With its stunning visuals and crisp sound quality, the Honor Magic V2 provides an exceptional multimedia experience.

5. Overall Value: If you're looking for a smartphone that offers a compelling combination of performance, features, and value, the Honor Magic V2 is hard to beat. With its premium design, innovative features, and competitive pricing, the Honor Magic V2 offers exceptional value for money compared to other flagship smartphones on the market.

In conclusion, whether you're a performance seeker, photography enthusiast, security-conscious user, multimedia enthusiast, or simply looking for overall value, the Honor Magic V2 has something to offer for everyone. With its impressive performance, versatile camera system, advanced security features, immersive multimedia experience, and exceptional value, the Honor Magic V2 is a smartphone that's worth considering for prospective buyers.

Appendix

In the appendix section, you'll find useful resources and information to further enhance your understanding of the Honor Magic V2 and its features.

1. Glossary of Technical Terms

To help you better understand the technical terms and jargon used throughout this book, here's a glossary of common terms:

- *OLED: Organic Light-Emitting Diode, a type of display technology that produces vibrant colors and deep blacks by emitting light directly from individual pixels.*
- *AMOLED: Active-Matrix Organic Light-Emitting Diode, a variation of OLED technology that uses an active*

matrix to control each pixel individually, resulting in improved brightness and efficiency.

- *Biometric Security: Security measures that use unique biological characteristics, such as fingerprints or facial features, for authentication and identification purposes.*

- *AI (Artificial Intelligence): Intelligence demonstrated by machines, such as smartphones, that mimic human cognitive functions, including learning, problem-solving, and decision-making.*

- *RAM: Random Access Memory, a type of computer memory that allows data to be accessed and manipulated quickly, often used for temporary storage of data and program instructions.*

- *GPU: Graphics Processing Unit, a specialized electronic circuit designed to rapidly manipulate and alter memory to accelerate the creation of images in a frame buffer for output to a display device.*
- *GPS: Global Positioning System, a satellite-based navigation system that provides location and time information to users anywhere on or near the Earth.*
- *NFC: Near Field Communication, a short-range wireless technology that allows devices to communicate with each other by touching or being in close proximity.*
- *HDR: High Dynamic Range, a technology that improves the contrast and color accuracy of images by*

capturing and displaying a wider range of brightness levels.